Amazing!

FROM CANCUN TO TULUM
QUINTANA ROO, MEXICO

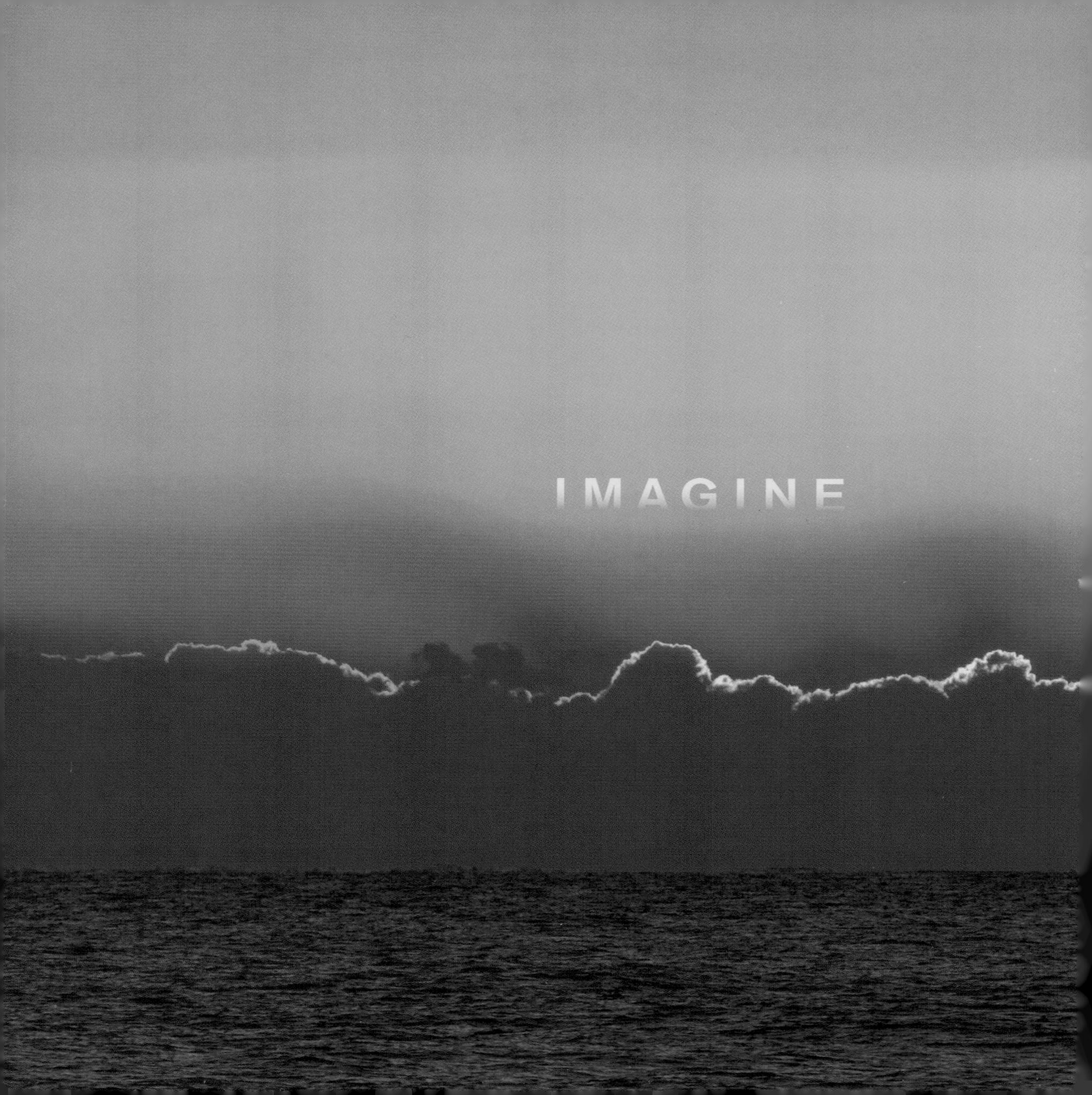
IMAGINE

journey

iNHALe

EXHALE

BALA

N C E

Peaceful

HARMONY

PARADISE

EXPLORE

HangOut

Caress

Encounter

ANCESTRAL

MYSTICAL

TIMELESS

YUCATAN'S WONDER

hug

INTENSE

Secluded

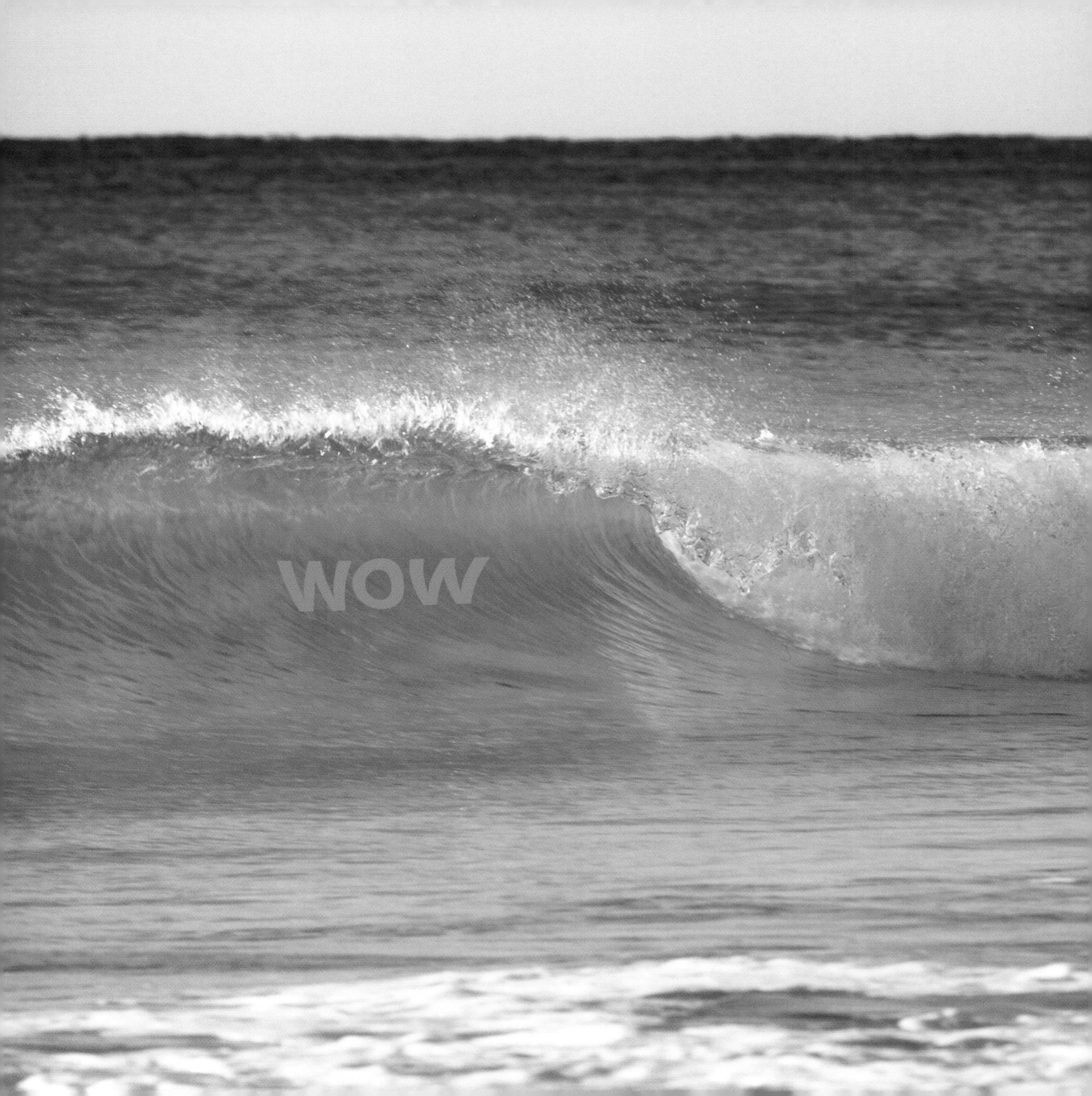
WOW

In love

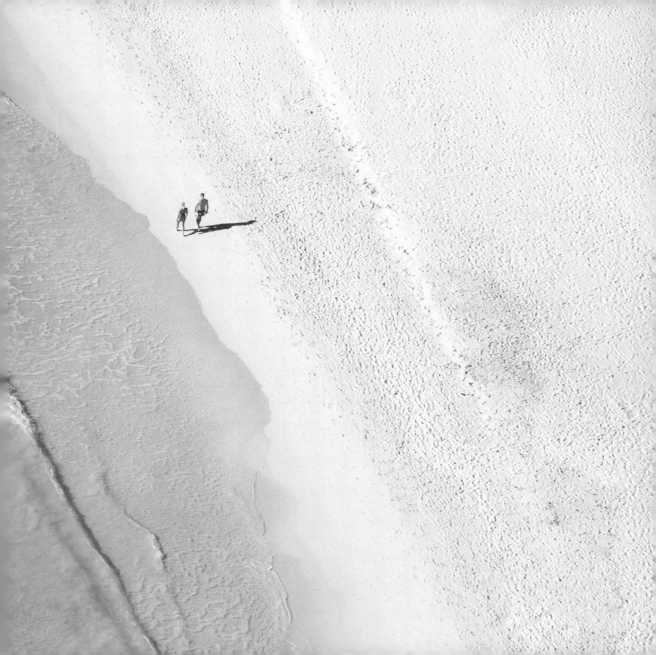

Pristine

Contemplate

NAMASTE

FLOAT

SPEED

Cool

dive

Discover

ADMIRE

ceviche

smile!

SEXY

salsa

Share

Exquisite

Delight

BLISS

Rhythm

dance

...to love

I do.

FIESTA!

Señorita

PLAY BALL

MISTY

Serene

One more day

in paradise

Gaze

Dream

PUBLISHERS

Ricardo Albin
David Cobar
Tamara Trottner

PHOTOGRAPHY

Demetrio Carrasco

COVER & ADDITIONAL
PHOTOGRAPHY

David Cobar
Río Secreto
Parque Xcaret
Parque Xel-Há
Parque Xplor
Hilario Itriago

DESIGN

Katya Villarreal

ISBN: 978-607-8128-38-9
Printed in Singapore
1st Edition. September 2013

Copyright Mexpapel Comercial S de RL de CV.

Contact: info@adoromexico.com

"Nunca dejes de volar"